Antonio Bresciani

The life of Abulcher Bisciarah

The little Angel of the Copts - Volume II

Antonio Bresciani

The life of Abulcher Bisciarah
The little Angel of the Copts - Volume II

ISBN/EAN: 9783741195990

Manufactured in Europe, USA, Canada, Australia, Japa

Cover: Foto ©Lupo / pixelio.de

Manufactured and distributed by brebook publishing software (www.brebook.com)

Antonio Bresciani

The life of Abulcher Bisciarah

THE LIFE

OF

ABULCHER BISCIARAH,

THE

"Little Angel of the Copts,"

AN

ALUMNUS OF THE ROMAN PROPAGANDA.

BY FATHER BRESCIANI,

AUTHOR OF "THE JEW OF VERONA."

Translated from the Italian,

WITH AN INTRODUCTION, BY
AUGUSTINE FRANCIS HEWIT,
PRIEST OF THE CONGREGATION OF THE MOST HOLY REDEEMER.

FILIUM MEUM EX EGYPTO VOCAVI.

VOLUME II.

New York:
P. O'SHEA, 739 BROADWAY.
M. DCCC. LVI.

Entered according to Act of Congress, in the year 1856,

BY P. O'SHEA,

In the Clerk's Office of the District Court of the United States for the Southern District of New York.

Printed and Stereotyped
By BILLIN & BROTHER, No. 20 North William Street,
New York.

Part the Second.

CHAPTER I.

ABULCHER RECEIVES THE HABIT OF THE ALUMNI OF THE PROPAGANDA—GOES THROUGH THE SPIRITUAL EXERCISES—COMMENCES THE STUDY OF GRAMMAR.

THE sixth of January, on which falls the Feast of the Epiphany of our Lord, has been selected as the most solemn festival of the Propaganda. Since the Church celebrates on that day the calling of the Gentiles to the knowledge of Christ, it is obviously most appropriate that these youths who are gathered together from all the nations of the globe, should observe it with a peculiar devotion and splendor. From the 28th of December they commence preparing themselves for it, by singing canticles and holy hymns, and celebrate the day itself with the greatest solemnity. The church of the College is open to the people from the first vespers of the vigil until the evening of the next day; and three bishops connected with the Sacred Congregation of the Propaganda, if they happen to be in Rome at the time, sing the mass, and the first and second vespers.

But that which chiefly attracts a great concourse of strangers, is the circumstance, that priests celebrate masses in all the rites of the Catholic Church; and it is a grand and beautiful spectacle to see sometimes at the five altars of the church, masses going on at the same time in the Armenian, Greek, Syrian, Chaldean, and Ethiopic or Coptic rites, with different vestments and ornaments, and with ceremonies all various, and all grave and sublime. This one chants in one tone, and another in a different one; one recites everything in an audible voice, and alternates with the clerk in the psalms and prayers; another offers up the holy mysteries in an inaudible tone: this one consecrates with leavened, and another with unleavened bread. A spectacle truly worthy of the Universal Church, an ever fruitful mother, and a queen variously adorned, and magnificent in her variegated splendor.

It was precisely on the day of this great festival that Abulcher received the grace to put on the habit of the collegians of the Propaganda. And, although no ceremony is observed, but every student puts on his habit in private, yet Abulcher, before he dressed himself in it, offered it up to the Blessed Virgin Mary, entreating her to bless it. He entreated her in the most tender manner, that she would never permit him to soil the glory of this habit with any sin, and especially with the stain of impurity. As he looked at his habit, which was seamed with red braid, and at the cingulum of a vermilion color with which it was bound, he considered this as the emblem of martyrdom; and, kissing it with ardor, he raised his eyes to a picture of the Blessed Virgin, and exclaimed: "Queen of Martyrs, I am ready. Here am I; send me—only make me worthy of this extraordinary grace." And, as he bound the crimson girdle about his waist, as it were the military sash which made him a knight of Christ, he promised, by the aid of Mary, to employ all his labors and studies to gain apostolic virtues. At the communion which he made with the other students in the chapel, he ratified anew this generous resolution, which he inviolably kept during the remainder of his life.

According to the ancient and established rule of the College, Abulcher should have first gone through the spiritual exercises, before receiving the habit. The reason for departing from this rule in his case was, that the Rector wished him to enjoy the happiness not only of being inscribed among the alumni of the Propaganda, but also of being adorned with their habit on the Feast of the Epiphany. Besides this, he was also extremely fatigued by his long journey; and the hardships of his sea voyage, together with the severe cold of the Appenines, which is extremely noxious to a native of a tropical climate, had given a rude shock to his constitution. All these circumstances determined his amiable and indulgent superior to dispense with the rule in his case.

As soon, however, as he thought himself somewhat restored, he desired ardently to recollect himself in God, and obtained permission to commence the sacred retirement of the exercises, which, according to the rule, lasts from eight to ten days. And as he understood neither Latin or Italian, a pious and experienced Coptic monk, who was living at Santo Stefano de Mori, was requested to instruct and guide him in the method of making his meditations.

Abulcher, as we have said already, had learned while he was still in Egypt, to meditate, from the light of the Holy Ghost Himself, who penetrated his heart from the earliest years of his boyhood; and he had nourished himself more and more daily with the strong and delicious food of prayer, which animated his soul to the acquisition of every virtue. And we have seen already how his heart was liquefied by that flame of divine love, and desired to be entirely consumed by it. His prayer was more the contemplation of a soul rapt and fixed in God, than a system or art of the spiritual life. But when his intellectual eye regarded the came to the meditation on The Kingdom of Christ. The loving invitation of his King to follow him everywhere, and his proposal to him to be always the first at the opening of the combat, the first to repel an assault, the first where the battle raged the most hotly, was the sharpest spur for the generous Abulcher. Therefore, he cast himself with humility on the ground, and promised, with magnanimous resolution, to follow him everywhere—exclaiming, "*Sequor te mi Jesu, sequor te quocumque ïeris:* it shall not suffice me to be enrolled under your standard, but throwing myself amongst the thickest of your enemies, I will combat by your side. I offer myself to you entirely, ready to fulfil your holy will in all things. And as I see that you wish that your followers should fight against sensuality, and against all carnal and earthly affections, I will contend against these enemies valiantly, and by your assistance will triumph over them."

He excited in himself continually anew these magnanimous sentiments, until he came to the wonderful meditation of The Two Standards. It seemed to him that he had promised his king and leader Jesus but little, in offering himself without reserve to his service; and, therefore, he concluded a solemn compact with him, that he would never rest until, having acquired the apostolic virtues by his education in the College, he had devoted himself entirely to the conversion of infidels.

And since the apostolic life brings with it fatigue, labor, and great self-contempt, and requires great strength of mind, in order to resist the attacks of the world, the flesh, and the devil; when he found his nature shuddering, and shrinking back from such great difficulties, he turned his eyes on Jesus, agonising in the garden at the simple view of the sufferings which awaited him. This sight gave him new courage, and he repeated with Jesus the words, *Pater, non mea sed tua voluntas fiat.* Considering then how savagely Jesus was persecuted by the Jews, and endured it all out of love to us, he offered himself to endure labors, calumnies, and persecutions, and even martyrdom, if that grace were accorded to him, out of love to Jesus, and for the salvation of souls.

Such were the holy resolutions which he made during his retreat. As he was well aware, however, that it is easy to make great and heroic promises to God, in a delightful meditation, and afar from all danger, he applied himself closely to discover the most powerful and certain means to assist him in bringing his resolutions into practice. And God, who enlightened him without ceasing, caused him to understand, that the only means of attaining such an arduous result, was to resign himself obediently to the conduct of his superiors, ready to fulfil their will in all things. In like manner he must observe punctually even the minutest rules of the College, if, as he was wont to say, those rules can be called minute, which are the causes of such great effects, and the beginning of such important results.

In point of fact, Abulcher gave, soon after his retreat, a proof of the sincerity of his oblation of himself to God and his superiors. For, having been placed in the lowest class of grammar, he applied himself so earnestly and attentively to learn those first elements, that his teacher gave him the highest praise. And, to speak the truth, the new scholars in the Propaganda have no easy task. Every one who reflects on the matter will see that it requires no little virtue to submit to that disagreeable, or, rather, tormenting exercise. For, as the pupils come from the most distant countries, and are generally past the age of boyhood, and their native languages are extremely diverse, in genius, form and construction, from the Latin and Italian, they have to overcome great difficulties in the beginning.

Abulcher proved his great patience, by overcoming, out of love to God, the protracted tedium of learning the grammar, and passed several months in spelling and pronouncing Latin and Italian words, before he came to the declension of nouns. He was very exact in studying his lessons, and, after the recitation, he used to beg of Tuchy to help him, promising him many rosaries and communions as a recompense. In order, however, that the dryness of these rudiments, and the weariness of so many hours of study in the class-room, and in his chamber, might not diminish his fervor in prayer, he was very careful not to subtract from it a single moment of the appointed time. In the written memoir of him, I find it recorded, that in order to practice humility, and to overcome his natural repugnance to that disagreeable study, he often went to his teacher, and begged him to punish him if he had not said his lesson well. He continued to do this in the higher class of grammar, with his beloved teacher, Don Andrea Nicolai, who has attested, "that Abulcher often presented himself with the air of one who had committed a fault, and did what I have never known any other to do, begged me to impose on him public penance for his faults, although he had not committed any, and, when his request was refused, he was quite disconsolate and afflicted." This is a true mark of singular virtue, such as was in former times exhibited by St. Ignatius, when he was learning the rudiments of grammar at Barcelona, in his thirty-third year.

CHAPTER II.

ABULCHER'S ZEAL IN THE OBSERVANCE OF THE RULES OF THE COLLEGE.

It is necessary that every one who consecrates himself to the apostolic life should break his own will at all times, and in all things, and conquer those repugnances which are so deeply seated in the natural feelings; he must become all things to all men, and retain nothing of himself, but, in a word, must bury the old man to rise again to a new life. The college of the Propaganda furnishes therefore to her students a palæstra in which they can exercise themselves beforehand in these different virtues. It is only necessary to reflect that they belong to many different nations, widely remote from each other, and equally separated by the difference of language, laws, customs, and climate, to understand partly how difficult it is for them to accommodate themselves in a short time, to one common rule and manner of life, and to become, as the Psalmist says, *unius moris in domo*. It is not easy to lay aside old habits; and those which one imbibes with his mother's milk, and which stamp their impress on his soul, when he first opens his eyes, and first comes to the use of reason, are usually so combined with the character of each individual, that they become a second nature.

Some are born in the soft and mild climate of Asia Minor, Greece, and Syria; others in the torrid zone, as the Ethiopians, Abyssinians, and natives of Guinea, Angola, and Congo; and others in the cold regions of Denmark, Sweden, Lower Canada, and Nova Scotia. Hence arises an infinite variety of complexions, manners, and customs—the easy, self-indulgent life of Asia, and the laborious, hard and self-denying life of the northern countries. At their first entrance into the Urban College, everything is new to the eye and the mind of the young alumni, many of whom, after embarking at the ports of their respective countries, never set foot on land until they arrive at Livorno, and from there come directly by Civita-Vecchia or Fiumicino to Rome. We can imagine what sensations of wonder arise in their minds, when they behold themselves suddenly transported from the most remote parts of the east or the west, into a country which in language, climate, manners, and costume, is so totally different from their own.

Let us take only the two extreme points. From the remotest part of the east we have Chinese; and they, who are accustomed in their social intercourse to an infinity of ceremonies, and conventional forms, and to reverences and prostrations without end, must regard the simple Italian manners as rude and unpolished. On the other hand, we have from the extreme west, a young Californian Indian, of the tribe of Checcegnajuis, who, accustomed to the forest, and to the free and simple life of the savage, must have seemed very strange and awkward in his own eyes, when he found himself here, buttoned up in a long and close soutane, and tied down to a regular life.

We have thrown out these preliminary observations, in order that we may render more manifest the virtue of the youth Abulcher, who set himself with such alacrity of spirit to overcome the repugnance which every one must feel in all its magnitude, when he is forced to accustom himself to such a novel mode of life. Whoever acts from love to God, however, finds every way smooth and plain, no matter how rough and uneven it may be.

Abulcher, who was animated by the most ardent desire to please his Lord, who had called him out of the depths of Egypt, in order to train him for the apostleship, desired that the rules might be shown to him, that he might observe them with the greatest exactness. It was customary in the Propaganda to assign to the new scholars one of the older and most edifying pupils, as a model and guide in the observance of the rule. Therefore Abulcher followed his guide in all things, (who was, probably, the same Tuchy mentioned before,) and by degrees learnt the rules, which he endeavored to keep as exactly as possible. Before all things, he manifested the greatest reverence for the companion assigned to him by the superiors, regarding him as his angel of counsel, and following his advice scrupulously. If he gave him but a sign in regard to his manner of behaving, he obeyed it instantly.

At the first stroke of the bell, he was at his chamber door, waiting until the Prefect gave the signal to go forward. While he was passing through the corridors, and over the stair-cases, he preserved the strictest silence, and a most composed and modest air.

He sprang out of bed at the first signal, although the season of the year was quite cold, and he, having been born in an extremely hot climate, felt the cold most sensibly. But he was so completely absorbed in God, that no suffering could draw him away from him in the least. The Prefects were accustomed, according to the rule, to visit the rooms after the pupils had retired to them, to see if the lights were put out at the appointed time. Abulcher, fearing lest he might not observe the signal, interrupted his prayer in the middle, undressed quickly, and extinguished his light, continuing then, as we shall see, to watch with God a long time afterward.

In the refectory he had ample opportunity to prove his spirit of mortification. Unaccustomed to our diet, he had not only to overcome his disrelish, but also the repugnance of the stomach for food to which it was unused. This necessity of eating food which does not agree with the system, often causes great suffering, and this is generally augmented in youths, by their imagination. Abulcher never manifested the slightest repugnance for the dishes that were set before him, but partook of all with a cheerful countenance, and as much apparent relish as if they had been the most delightful viands in the world. And let no one believe that the healthy appetite of a youth makes him indifferent to the quality of his food. For experience shows that nothing is so difficult in an institute of education, as to arrange the table to the satisfaction of all. And this is especially the case where the students are from many different nations, each having their particular tastes, and their favorite dishes.

If the students of the Propaganda were allowed an indiscriminate use of their native languages, it would be turned into a perfect Babel, and the studies and discipline would suffer greatly. It is, therefore, prescribed with great wisdom, by the rules, that every one must speak Latin or Italian, while, at the same time, they are allowed to speak their mother-tongue at certain times, and in certain places, that they may not forget it. Abulcher did his best to comply with this rule, in order not to deviate in any respect from the general custom. Therefore, he was very attentive in the hours of recreation to learn new words; he asked continually the meaning of this or that word, and the names of different objects; and he remembered, and made use of, everything which he learned. In a short time he could speak a little, and as soon as he could make himself understood tolerably well, he dropped his Arabic altogether, and confined himself to the Italian, in order to observe the rule.

As every one was obliged to make his own bed, sweep his room, and keep it in order, in order to get accustomed to a missionary life, Abulcher was very attentive to this point, and delighted to keep his room a very pattern of neatness and good order; and, from the appearance of his room, one might easily conclude that a similar order and purity reigned in the interior chamber of his soul. Indeed, in all his manners there was a certain gravity and maturity, combined with such an amiable suavity, that he attracted all to himself. He was humble, meek, and gentle, and avoided gossip and idle talk. That mean envy and malignity which is wounded by the success of others, found no place in his breast. He was always anxious to advance in virtue and learning, without regarding who was before or behind him; and he kept himself always in the presence of God, with the sole intention of pleasing him in all things. He was not quarrelsome, or given to murmuring, or impolite; but accessible to all, open, gay, and ingenuous in his bearing. No one ever saw him vexed by an untoward accident, or a bitter word which was spoken to him by another; on the contrary, if he could do it, without displeasing still more his companion, he returned it with a soft word, or a courteous action. If any one in the recreation commenced making sport of another, he went away under some fair pretext, not because he was an enemy to pleasantry, for he was himself facetious and witty, but because he believed that this ridicule and mimicry of others was attended with the danger of offending them, and violating charity. He fled the company of tattlers, knowing from the teaching of God's Word, that an ill regulated tongue easily says things which had better be left unsaid.

He never touched the person of another, even in sport, because both modesty and the rule forbade it. And as the rule prescribes that when the alumni meet each other, they shall make an inclination of the head, without speaking, Abulcher, whenever he met a fellow student in the corridors, took off his biretum, and passed by; and, if the other attempted to speak with him, he smiled graciously, and made a gesture, which seemed to say, "I would gladly speak with you, but I cannot." His companions were never offended by this conduct, for they knew that he was an exact observer of the rule.

Abulcher acted in a similar manner when he went into the school, where pupils from different museums are assembled, and where talking is strictly forbidden. He went to his place in silence, and if the professor had not yet arrived, and any one asked him a question, he would not answer it, even if it related to the lesson, but fixed his eyes on his book, and repeated his task. His companions were extremely edified by this conduct, and they respected his virtue so much, that they not only ceased to trouble him by talking to him in the school, but his simple presence, and the gravity and dignity of his demeanor had such an effect upon them, that they acted in a similar manner themselves.

He never set his foot within the chamber of another, and if any one rapped at his door, he went immediately, and, opening it half way, dismissed his visitor with as much politeness, and as few words as possible. He never went into the offices, or spoke with the servants, and if he wanted anything for himself, he did not ask for it in person, but applied to his Prefect for it.

The esteem and veneration which he manifested for his superiors, showed clearly that he regarded them as holding the place of God, and that he was convinced that in obeying them, he rendered obedience to God himself, who has solemnly declared, *Qui vos audit me audit.* Don Giovanni Gravio, who was his Prefect for four years, and whose testimony we shall often have occasion to cite, was accustomed to say, that he was never found by his companions, or masters, or superiors, transgressing the smallest precept, or rule, or custom, or private advice, either of the Rector or of himself.

In all the practices of piety, he had no one who came near him in fervor and exactness.

In the morning, as soon as he was dressed, and had made his bed, he recited very devoutly the Little Hours of the Office of the Blessed Virgin, which are prescribed by the rule. After this, he went, with his soul entirely recollected in God, to the domestic oratory, to make, in common with his companions, a meditation of half an hour, which he passed in sweet colloquies with his Lord; taking care, however, to moderate his acts of love in such a way, that they should not force from him involuntary sighs and sobs, which would attract the attention and admiration of those around him. Whenever he was among his companions, he avoided carefully every singularity, and remained perfectly still, with his head gently inclined. Those who were opposite to him, whenever they looked at him, felt their hearts inflamed with the love of God; and declared, that to look at Abulcher meditating, was a powerful means of becoming recollected, and banishing distractions.

At mass he remained with his eyes immovably fixed on the priest, as if his soul were borne up to God in a sweet rapture; and his face glowed from the burning ardor of his soul, which was sometimes at the time of the elevation, so vehement that his forehead was bathed in a profuse perspiration.

When the recreation after dinner was finished, he recited the vespers and compline of the Little Office of the Blessed Virgin; and after the school (the daily walk having not then been introduced), he went in silence to his chamber, and recited his matins and lauds with great devotion.

Without going any further into these minute details, it is enough to observe, that Abulcher was always guided by the maxim, *Qui timet Deum nihil negligit;* and avoided with the greatest care even the smallest faults and imperfections.

In order that he might more rapidly advance in virtue, he had frequent conferences with his spiritual father, Don Ignazio Oliva, a man of great virtue, and a fine discernment in the things of God, who was most zealous in promoting among the students, piety, mortification, and every part of that high perfection, at which young men destined to an apostolical life ought to aim. He was Abulcher's confessor and spiritual father, during the whole time of his residence in the College, and from him we have many most valuable testimonials of his eminent virtue, and of the baptismal innocence with which his blessed soul was adorned from the cradle to the grave.

CHAPTER III.

ABULCHER TAKES THE OATH OF THE MISSIONS—FRUIT WHICH HE DERIVES FROM A VISITATION OF THE POPE.

THESE were only the first essays which Abulcher made, in order to run afterwards in earnest on the difficult path of the apostolic life. His vigorous soul never lost its strength or courage. Disregarding all the hindrances thrown in his way by the rage of the enemy, the allurements of the flesh, and the resistance of that law in us which is always hostile to virtue, he pursued a direct course towards the sublime goal which was set before him. He made such rapid progress, and passed over so much ground, that at every step he felt himself lighter and more free, and God strengthened him continually with new and more abundant graces, as he is accustomed to do with his courageous and faithful servants.

Eight months had now elapsed since his entrance into the College, and his holy conversation, and the spotless purity of his soul, had won for him to such a degree the reverence of his companions, and the love and esteem of his superiors, that Cardinal Petra determined to permit him at once to make the oath of the missions.

This is a solemn oath, made before the altar, in the hands of a prelate, by which the subject binds himself to receive holy orders, to devote himself for life to the missions, under the jurisdiction of the Propaganda, and to fulfil certain other prescribed conditions bearing on the principal obligation.

When Monsignor Forteguerri had informed Bisciarah that he must prepare himself to take this oath, the pious youth went immediately to Don Ignazio Oliva, and begged him to instruct him fully in its nature, and in the best manner of preparing himself to make it. After receiving a full instruction on these points from the wise and experienced priest, Abulcher commenced preparing himself for this important act, by prayers, penances, and a strict retreat of several days, in order to obtain from God the strength necessary to accomplish such an arduous work as the conversion of infidels. On the 29th of September, 1732, the Feast of St. Michael the Archangel, Abulcher went very early to the church, and casting himself down before a beautiful bas relief statue of the archangel, which is at the left hand of the high altar, prayed, with tears, for a long time, that he would condescend to present in person the oath he was about to take, before the throne of the Almighty, that it might be more agreeable to his Divine Majesty. That he, as the defender and champion of the Catholic Church, would deign to attest the sincerity of his oblation, and the loyalty of his soul, in swearing to cherish no other desire in his heart, except to devote himself to the mission of Egypt, and the welfare and salvation of that country. That he, as the prince of the Lord's host, would extend his shield over him, and receive on it all the blows which the infernal enemy, animated with fury against all who seek to rescue souls from his grasp, should aim at him. Protected by this shield, he was ready to engage in any combat.

The time being arrived, Monsignor Forteguerri said mass, and communicated Abulcher. When he had finished mass, and laid aside his vestments, he sat down on a faldstool, and one of the oldest students read in a loud voice the bull of Pope Alexander VII., and afterwards, simultaneously with Abulcher, the formula of the oath. When they came to these words, *Voveo, et juro, quod jussu prædictæ Congregationis de Propaganda Fide, sine mora in provinciam meam revertar, ut ibi perpetuo in divinis administrandis laborem meum ac operam pro salute animarum impendam:* "I vow, and swear, that when commanded by the Congregation de Propaganda Fide, I will return directly to my province, and there labor perpetually in the sacred ministry for the salvation of souls;" a smile of joy gleamed on the countenance of Abulcher, and he repeated several times, "yes, my God! *impendam, impendam.*" Then, kneeling down before his lordship, he laid his hand on the Gospel, and took the oath, while the sweetest tears trickled from his eyes; and many of his companions, moved to devotion, could not contain themselves from weeping with him.

During the same year, Pope Clement XII.,

a great favorer of the College, appointed a solemn visitation, for which he selected the four cardinals, Barberino, Pico, Spinola, and Petra. And, as almost a century had now passed since the foundation of the College, he directed these cardinals to subject the constitution, and the whole method of management and government in the College, to a narrow scrutiny, in order to make such changes and improvements as they deemed necessary. These commands of the Pope were strictly followed, and at the end of the visitation, the rules, with the changes and additions made by the cardinals, were published by the press of the Sacred Congregation, and given into the hands of the alumni to be observed.

Abulcher, who, during the visitation, had pleased the cardinals uncommonly, by his extraordinary piety and modesty, resolved anew to strive after Christian perfection, by following the shortest and most certain road, viz., by observing most exactly all the new rules established by the Sacred Congregation. And in this he had two noble motives. The first was to please God, and fulfil the oath which he had sworn before the altar on the Holy Gospels, and the second was to assist his fellow students, by his example, to pay a ready and cheerful obedience to the commands of their superiors.

In order that he might better understand the sublimity of his vocation, and the intentions of the holy Church in calling him into the Urban College, he read over often that part of the preface to the rules, which follows:

"What care, what application and diligence, should not the Sacred Congregation of the Propaganda employ in admitting and instructing the youths who compose the Urban College. The Holy See has selected it, not for the benefit of a few dioceses, but for the advantage of almost an entire world, which is either deprived of the light of the Gospel, as is the case in the vast regions where Paganism and Mohammedanism reign, or, having formerly possessed this light, have been buried anew in the fearful darkness of heresy and schism. This is no seminary for the education of ordinary ecclesiastics, but of *apostles*, whose office is, as every one knows, the most holy, the most elevated, and the most perfect. Out of it must come those zealous and valiant warriors, who not only encounter with a firm and serene countenance, the dangers and obstacles which oppose the preaching of the faith of Jesus Christ, but who rejoice at chains and exile, at prisons, and death itself. It is a seminary, in fine, in which the greatest virtues ought to be common and familiar, and where faults should be very trivial, and always corrected as soon as they are seen."

Such is the language of the preface.

The reading of this inflamed the heart of Abulcher with the most ardent desire to acquire the virtues of an apostle; and this was not a mere ebullition of youthful enthusiasm, but a firm, unwearied, and persevering zeal, which, instead of diminishing, increased constantly, as long as he lived, as we shall see in the next following chapter.

CHAPTER IV.

ABULCHER'S PROGRESS IN PERFECTION—HIS HUMILITY, MODESTY, AND ABSTINENCE.

WHAT has already been said of the virtues of Abulcher, might seem in the eyes of many, whose knowledge of spiritual things is limited, more than sufficient to justify us in calling him a saint. He who strives, however, after genuine sanctity, will never be satisfied because he has done a great deal; but, on the contrary, that which seems something great to those whose spiritual insight is limited, appears to him as very little, or absolutely nothing. So it was with Abulcher. Hitherto we have seen in him only a youth of large desires. And although he had already advanced so far in the observance of the rules, in continence, and in the love of virtue, that he might justly be called a perfect model of a Propagandist, nevertheless, his magnanimous and robust spirit aspired to things incomparably more sublime and arduous. He was always looking at the heights above him; and it was his constant maxim, that although obedience, diligence, and piety, were sufficient to make one a good student, yet, in order to become an apostle, it was necessary to practice beforehand, like a soldier in his barracks, the exercises of the most exalted perfection.

That was the least part of his excellence which was manifested in his exterior conduct. All his efforts were directed to the formation of that interior habit of sanctity, from which exterior works derive all their nerve and virtue. He saw, by a clear inward light from God, that the apostolical life, unless based on solid virtue, is exposed to the most dangerous occasions of falling. The missionary's solitary position, where there are no witnesses of his actions, and where he is cut off from all counsel and spiritual aid, in the midst of heathens whose privation of faith has drawn them into the most vile and abominable customs, the mild and enervating climate, the dangerous examples and temptations which surround him, the license of manners, which has become inveterate by the lapse of ages, and has come to be regarded, if not as entirely innocent, yet as exempt from all gross culpability, together with the inward spark of concupiscence, which is not extinguished even in those who are consecrated to the most holy works; these are dangers which require that a missionary should be armed with a more than human virtue. This virtue is something which is not to be obtained for a price, or received as a gift from the superiors when one departs for the mission; but it descends into the soul as a gratuitous gift of God, when it is sought for by constant prayer; and when once given, it is retained by the powerful aid of grace, and by continual exercise. For example, God grants the gift of humility, but it is ordinarily preserved only by reiterated acts of interior and exterior humiliation; and the more a person practices himself in acts of humility, the more humble he will become. The same is true of every virtue; and because Abulcher desired to possess all the virtues, therefore he exercised himself in all.

His penetrating eye did not pass over that primary virtue, which every one must acquire who desires perfection, viz., humility. This virtue does not consist in saying things greatly in dispraise of one's self, as is customary with many who possess but a moderate degree of virtue, or none at all, and who say these things with the idea that nobody believes them, hoping to draw praise and honor out of their self-abasement. · Humility consists in the knowledge of one's own proper nothingness, whence arises a low esteem of ourselves, and the desire of the low esteem of others. The truly humble person even seeks for opportunities of appearing foolish and ignorant, and when he has found them, rejoices as much as a worldly man when he is esteemed as wise and powerful.

Abulcher, who aimed at reaching this high degree of humility, began by begging of God light to know how poor he was in all natural and supernatural goods. He considered himself as an extremely sinful and ungrateful youth, in comparison with the rich and admirable benefits which the liberal hand of God had lavished upon him from his childhood. And considering himself poor and miserable, he would never accept of any praise from his companions, not even from his most intimate and familiar friends. He always took the last place; and if the esteem and veneration which his companions cherished for him were at any time manifested by some action honorable to himself, he blushed, became confused, and retired to some secret place. On the contrary, if any one, annoyed by his reserved manners, spoke rudely to him, or contrived to place him in a mortifying position, he was rejoiced at it, and regarded this individual as a signal benefactor, and one who had a correct opinion of his worthlessness.

While he attributed all his imperfections to himself alone, as to a centre of all evil, and a fountain of every kind of sin, he referred the glory of every good action to God, the sole fountain of all excellence. From his first awaking in the morning, he looked towards God, and expected every succor from him, offering up to him all his thoughts, affections, and actions, during the day, with the intention not to do anything which he did not refer to his glory. He renewed this pure intention before each single work and action, even those which are trivial, and he reaped two great advantages from this practice. The first was, that even his most trivial actions, being referred to the glory of God, lost their insignificance, and became truly great, while, on the contrary, great deeds, not performed for God, lose all worth and grandeur. The second was, that by this practice, he prepared himself to perform his future labors for the salvation of souls in the missionary life, with the same purity of intention. A missionary is exposed to continued distractions: journeys, caravans, voyages, negotiations, business affairs, the arrangement of marriages, the visitation of the sick, the burial of the dead, the instruction of neophytes, controversies with

Protestants, disputations with schismatics, adjudication of disputes, the detection of insidious schemes, fatigues, solicitudes, pains, and anxieties in countless numbers. Amid such a confusion of affairs, the mind being drawn in every direction, becomes so estranged from itself, that without the sweet and powerful habit of raising itself to God by a pure intention, it is in danger of being carried away by the current of human accidents, without obtaining any advantage except a tumultuous and useless activity. Hence it happens sometimes, that young missionaries being drawn into the vortex, so far from accomplishing that noble end which they have proposed for themselves, make shipwreck of their own souls, and forfeit their eternal crown.

As Abulcher labored only for God, so he sought only after God, and practised the recollection of the Divine Presence with such fidelity, that he never lost sight of it for a moment, no matter how intently he might be occupied. *Quærite Dominum et confortamini, quærite faciem ejus semper.* This was the favorite lesson which he was wont to inculcate on his young companions, when they requested him to speak with them of spiritual things. We shall see a little later with what lively earnestness he inculcated it on the young Swedish student, Roll, who was a great friend of his.

That he might not be distracted from the presence of God, he remained in the solitude of his beloved chamber, which he seldom left, unless the signal of obedience, or the duty of charity, called him out. In order to recall frequently to his memory the presence of God, he prepared a little tablet, on which he wrote in large letters, "REMEMBER THAT GOD SEES YOU," and hung it up over his desk; and every time he looked at it, he repeated his favorite ejaculation, "*Deus, Deus meus, amote.* After his death, Don Giovanni Gravio, who was a great admirer of his virtue, took possession of it, in the general seizure which the students made of the effects of their late saintly companion, and always prized it most highly as a relic of that innocent servant of God, and as a faithful witness of his great care to keep himself always in the Divine Presence. We have already seen, that from his childhood in Sethfeh, all creatures reminded him of God, that he breathed only for God, and lived only in his pure love.

As a guard over his virginal purity, he had placed (as we have read of St. Aloysius Gonzaga,) an angelical modesty and the most exact vigilance over all the emotions of his heart. Whether he was in or out of the house, he never raised his eyes from the ground. In conversation with his most familiar friends he kept his head always bent in a modest and graceful manner, so that what he did in order to preserve the spotless purity of his soul, seemed to be simply the effect of natural timidity. Even when he was taking the most retired and lonely walks, he preserved the same exterior composure, and a reserve full of gravity and sweetness; and he did not lay it aside even when he was entirely alone in his chamber.

On festivals, and during vacations, the students were accustomed to go for recreation to the Villa de Medici, which is now the French Academy. There they recreated their minds, fatigued by study, with various sports and amusements, and passed delightfully the afternoon hours amid the delicious groves, in the shady recesses, and under the green luxuriant hedges, indulging in all the gaiety of youthful and buoyant spirits. Some of them wandered through a grove of laurels to the summit of a hill which rises above the tops of the trees, where you see all Rome lying at your feet, and enjoy the most magnificent view of the city, with its hills, its palaces, its pyramids, temples, and gardens. This beautiful prospect, which is more like the fabled works of enchantment than reality, is justly considered as the greatest wonder of the Medici Villa. But the refined modesty of Abulcher, combined with the most severe spirit of mortification, would never permit him to feast his eyes on this innocent and sublime spectacle.

Don Andrea Nicolai, his master, often went out to this villa, to enjoy the pious and devout conversation of Abulcher. He did not seek him in those places where he heard the merry shouts of laughter, and the noise of running, and other kinds of sport, but entering softly into the thickest recesses of the wood, he went on, looking carefully on every side, for the hiding place of his dear pupil. Along the edge of this grove is a green meadow, solitary and quiet, where the perfect silence is interrupted only by the mournful chirping of the little birds, and here he usually found him either kneeling or sitting down, with his chaplet in his hand, or absorbed in holy contemplations. This sight moved the good priest to devotion, and approaching Abulcher, he began to hold sweet converse with him on the divine perfections, the only subject for which he had any taste. He has left us his testimony, that Abulcher never showed any taste for any conversation except on God and celestial things.

If Abulcher did not allow his eyes the liberty of looking at the innocent prospects of the country, and of gardens, for his delight and recreation, we may easily conclude how great was the jealousy with which he guarded them from looking on other objects which might in the slightest degree contaminate his purity. Therefore, at the Medici Villa, where the walks, the fountains, and the grottoes, are decorated with the most beautiful statues, both ancient and modern, he would never look at one of them, because he knew that some of them were not modest. He did the same at the villas of the Roman princes and nobles, where nature and art rival each other in the most wonderful manner, but where often the beauty of the statues and pictures is much more striking than their propriety.

Such being the strict guard which Abulcher kept over his eyes, and over all his senses and emotions, it is no wonder that he preserved his baptismal innocence intact until his death. We have already seen how exact was his vigilance during the whole period of his boyhood at Sethfeh, and how he redoubled it on his voyage to Rome, and never relaxed it afterwards. The merit of this extraordinary modesty was greatly heightened by the fact, that he was in no wise melancholy, or of an unamiable and harsh disposition, but friendly, affable, easy and polite in his manner with all; preserving always a serene countenance, lighted up with an expression of modest gaiety and kindliness. He took great care to preserve these natural gifts, knowing well how different the modesty of missionaries is from that of hermits, since the latter are obliged by their vocation to preserve their modesty by shunning all intercourse with men, while the former are bound to make use of theirs to win the confidence of their fellow men, and to preserve themselves from the seductive illusions of the world.

Behold the shield with which Abulcher defended his innocence until death. Another powerful weapon with which he defended this celestial virtue was temperance. He was always extremely spare in his diet even from boyhood, but in the Urban College he practised the virtue of temperance to such an extreme, that it deserved rather the name of abstinence; for we read of him, that besides the fasts common to all, he often contented himself at the table with nothing but *minestra* * and fruit. This abstinence in a youth who was in the full vigor of his age, and growing rapidly, is rather to be admired than imitated. St. Aloysius Gonzaga used to do the same, and plead his delicate constitution as an excuse for his protracted fasts. So, also, Abulcher, as his memoirs relate, used to conceal his mortification, by ascribing his frequent abstinences to his care to preserve his extremely feeble health.

To all these industrious efforts he added

* A kind of Italian soup, commonly the first dish served in ecclesiastical and religious houses.—Tr.

repeated and most minute examinations during the day, in which he scrutinized every thought and interior movement, weighed every word, and judged every action, to see if it was proper, grave, and modest, and if nothing had insinuated itself which could defile, or even cast a shadow upon his spotless soul. Not satisfied with this minute attention to himself, he studied the lives of Jesus Christ, the Blessed Virgin, and the saints, in order to discover constantly new modes of perfecting himself, and to perceive, by comparing himself with these models, where there was something to be pruned away, where something was to be added or reformed. Then the reading of the Imitation of Christ, by Thomas à Kempis, which he kept always by him, was of immense advantage to him; and he fed his mind and heart on it as with the most delicious food, full of nutriment to strengthen the spirit, and make it firm and robust in the most masculine virtues.—A little book with which every missionary ought to be familiar, as containing the most exalted precepts and admonitions to the most consummate apostolical perfection.

CHAPTER V.

OF ABULCHER'S EXTRAORDINARY SPIRIT OF MORTIFICATION AND PENANCE.

THE rigorous scrutiny to which Abulcher subjected everything which passed in his mind, or fell under the cognizance of his senses, leads us to speak of the absolute mastery which he exercised over his passions. A person is only master over anything in so far as he possesses it; but the passions cannot be possessed with a perfect dominion, rebellious

LIFE OF ABULCHER BISCIARAH. 175

as they are in their nature, unless they have first been combated and subjugated. This combat is a severe and a protracted one; for the enemy is obstinate, his artifices are most subtle, and his stratagems infinite. This is a perpetual war which a man must wage with himself, and he who comes out conqueror, and brings his passions into absolute subjection, is pronounced by the Holy Ghost to be more glorious and more valiant than the heroes who have conquered cities.

Abulcher was always in a hostile attitude against these domestic enemies; but being prevented from his earliest childhood by celestial illuminations, he knew from the outset that he must attack them before they became strong, deeply rooted, and contumacious. Therefore, he clipped their wings while they were young, and put them in fetters, treating them as slaves and prisoners, and resolved that reason, as their born queen, should rule them at pleasure. The means he employed to make them subject and submissive were, to seek to find them out, and when he had found them, to persecute them without mercy. He always did precisely the contrary of that which they desired, by a continual self-denial; he refused them everything which they liked, and forced them to take up with those things which they most abhorred. He never showed them a friendly countenance, or treated them in any other way than as slaves; and thus he subdued them so completely to his own will, that they even assisted him to overcome the arduousness of certain of the more sublime virtues. In this way he imitated those experienced pilots who know how to turn contrary winds in their own favor by skilful tacking.

By dint of long study in abnegation and mortification, he had acquired such empire over himself, that he had not only in great measure blunted his sensibility, but what is more difficult, had detached his mind from every earthly affection. And, although his beloved mission of Egypt was the only object of his aspirations, he nevertheless possessed a perfect liberty of spirit in God, entirely indifferent whether the right or left bank of the Nile was assorted to him by Divine Providence as the theatre of his labors. After he had left his country, his parents, and friends, he regarded himself as dead to them all, and never thought of them except to recommend them to God, for the love of whom he had made this entire sacrifice. Therefore, says the MSS., he was observed to be entirely detached from his paternal house and all earthly affections, and to have his thoughts exclusively fixed on heaven. He saw clearly that a missionary who still nourishes the germs of natural affection for his relations, and is occupied in laying plans to elevate them in rank and fortune, is no apostle, but a merchant. And the holy fathers, while they compare the true apostle to the royal eagle who sweeps in freedom through the air in rapid circles, wherever the impetuosity of his soaring desires carries him, liken the missionary, who is greedy of gain, to the tortoise, who, burdened with the house which presses down his back, can scarcely drag himself along, and is hardly able to pull his feet out of the mud where they are sticking.

After the first year which Abulcher passed in Rome, he became grievously ill, and it is impossible to describe the patience and constancy with which he suffered the excruciating tortures caused by an obstinate retention of urine. But in the greatest severity of his sufferings, he never complained, and when he was questioned by his companions, he replied, with a tranquil countenance, "Let us thank the Lord." The necessity of submitting to surgical operations was far more intolerable to the modest youth, than all the spasms of his malady; therefore, he could only be induced to consent to it by obedience, and his only consolation was to reflect that our Lord Jesus Christ suffered in a similar manner, from love of us, on the cross. During the surgical operation, he controlled his agony with such firmness of spirit, that he would not use any means of support or relief, except to raise his eyes to heaven, or to fix them on a crucifix. Thus the MSS.

He had often violent pains in the stomach, which caused him great suffering and languor, especially for some hours after dinner. With this was connected an extreme weakness of the chest and a deeply-seated dry cough, which, as we shall see, never left him until it brought him to the grave. His paroxysms of coughing were so violent, that the poor youth was often completely exhausted, and spit blood in large quantities. Yet the serenity of his countenance was unalterable, and amid these great sufferings he joyfully blessed God, who deigned to allow him to taste the sweetness of his cross. And as he always had the spirit of observance at heart, he concealed his maladies as much as possible, in order not to be compelled by the physicians to use those singularities which he disliked so much. Therefore, as the MS. memoir tells us, he never sought to relieve himself by any particular indulgences in regard to food, or asked for dispensation from the most exact observance of the rules. He was most prompt even in the coldest weather to rise early in the morning, and go to chapel, to the meditation of the Community; and on holidays, knowing that the Rector and the physician wished him to go out and take the air, he never asked leave to stay in the house, although at times he was so weak that every movement caused him pain and fatigue, and he could not go up or down stairs without the assistance of his companions.

He continued his studies, as far as possible, without intermission, and when he had no longer strength to fix his eyes or his thoughts on the book, he recalled his wandering mind and compelled it to apply itself anew, by the mere force of his unbending will. And since the testimony of his Prefect and companions on this point is the most authentic, I quote, as I have already frequently done, the very words of the MSS.

No inconvenience or weakness could ever induce him to diminish his great application to study, which he made in order to acquire a sufficient capital of learning so necessary to an evangelical laborer, who must enlighten the minds of those who are sitting in the darkness and shadow of death. As he was not able to remain long at his desk, on account of the weakness of his chest, which was affected by the disease which brought him finally to the grave, he fixed a standing desk on the wall of his chamber, where he studied for hours together, with great inconvenience, which he cheerfully endured without a murmur; and he never swerved from his generous purpose during six years, in which time, by extraordinary exertions, he finished the courses of Grammar and Rhetoric, and a part of his Philosophy.

Notwithstanding Abulcher was afflicted with so many maladies, which diminished his vital forces and caused him such severe sufferings that the Prefect Gravio used to compare him to the patient Job, yet, as if these were not sufficient to preserve the innocence of his heart, he added to them many others with his own hand. And whenever any one wished to persuade him to give up at least in part his penances, he answered with deep feeling, that Jesus, crucified for love of us, deserves as a recompense at least some little offering on our part, to attest our desire of imitating him in his sufferings.

He provided himself with a catenella of iron, armed with sharp points, which he bound about his loins, and never took off, day or night, wearing it even when he was confined to bed by sickness, and thus added to the pains which he endured in the reins and stomach, the punctures of these points, which lacerated and covered with blood his innocent flesh. Some of his companions having discovered this on a certain occasion, informed the Prefect, who, not being able to endure the thought of his suffering so much, went to visit him in his room, and earnestly entreated him to take pity on himself, and to lay aside this painful cilicium during his sickness. Abulcher bowed his head and obeyed.

The alumni of the Propaganda were accustomed to take the discipline every Friday evening, in memory of the passion and death of the Lord. Abulcher, however much he might be suffering, never failed to go to the chapel, to listen to the discourse which the spiritual father made before the discipline; and afterwards he scourged himself severely. And, as if this penance was too little to satisfy his thirst for suffering, Don Giovanni Gravio attests, that while his companions were sound asleep, in the deepest silence of the night, Abulcher disciplined himself with such force, that he was moved to a tender devotion, and listened for a long time to the severe blows with which the innocent youth chastised his body, and to the deep and moving sighs with which he accompanied this rigid penance.

All these austerities, joined to the interior mortification which kept him always on the watch, and employed in scrutinizing whatever passed in his mind, and regulating his exterior actions, undermined continually his health, while they purified his spirit in a wonderful manner. And therefore it is to be believed, that Don Ignazio Oliva, his spiritual father, was directed by an extraordinary light from God, in permitting to such an emaciated invalid as he was, fasts, penances, and other austerities, severe enough to injure the constitution of the most robust youth. But God works in his saints in the most wonderful ways, which often escape the ken of mortals; and we must be satisfied to admire his ways without understanding them, knowing that he will always bring about our own greater good, and his own greater glory.

CHAPTER VI.

ABULCHER'S LOVE FOR HIS COMPANIONS, AND HOW HE EXCITED THEM TO FERVOR, BY HIS WORDS AND BY HIS EXAMPLE.

SUCH great virtue could not exist without charity, which is the vital spark of all good works. We shall see how vivid and ardent it was in the soul of Abulcher. He regarded his companions as brothers; and beholding in them only the image of God, he reverenced it in each one, without regard to their attainments in science or virtue. Of whatever nation they might be, they were equally dear to him. The accidental circumstance of being a native of a northern or a southern clime, did not affect his sentiments towards them in the least, but he was always ready to oblige all whenever he had an opportunity.

And since, as it usually happens in a collection of youth out of several different nations, every one following his natural love of country, preferred his own nation to all others, Abulcher, in order to avoid useless contests, never spoke of Egypt. Whenever one of his fellow-students was ridiculed by his companions, on account of the customs of his nation, which they called over-strained and ludicrous, he defended him by saying that foreigners cannot judge national customs correctly. A certain usage seems ridiculous to one, which in the eyes of another is noble and grave; and one will consider that rudeness, which passes with others for the most consummate politeness. Nations have their peculiar usages, as languages have theirs; and whoever would attempt to judge of these merely by the sound of the words, or the shape of the letters, without understanding the sense, would act in a foolish and childish manner, unworthy of a man of sense.

When any one declaimed on the power and celebrity of his nation, and the others boastfully opposed to him the greater glory of their own, Abulcher, who was witty and facetious, was accustomed to terminate the dispute by saying, in a pleasant manner: "Do keep quiet! We Orientals dispute about our ancient nobility, just like decayed gentlemen of old families. Each one of us has been great, and lorded it over the others in turn; but now nothing remains to any of us of our famous conquests, except the rod of the Mohammedans, which keeps us all in misery and servitude."

When he was out walking, he did not care whether he had a Syrian or a Chaldean as his companion; but he was satisfied with any one who was assigned to him, and conversed readily with every one without exception. His piety caused him to prefer the society of the most devout, with whom he could freely converse about God; but he preferred charity and obedience to his own pleasure. He was easy and affable with all, yet he had certain holy artifices of his own, by which he skilfully led the conversation to holy things, without his companion perceiving it. And when he saw that his companion relished some of his observations, his fervor was kindled to such a degree that the other caught the flame of his enthusiasm. When the conversation ran on his favorite theme, of the sublimity and sanctity of the apostolic vocation, he gave utterance to such striking conceptions, and such vivid and forcible arguments, that the students acknowledged that they were more moved by them, than by any sermons, or spiritual books.

At the arrival of new students in the College, he met them with a most friendly air, and was very officious in procuring for them every necessary and comfort. If he was unable to speak their language, yet his expressive eyes manifested his tender affection for them, and the very sight of him drove away that sadness and heaviness of heart with which the new comers were usually oppressed, on being transported into such novel and unaccustomed scenes.

Whenever one of the alumni, having finished his studies, was ordained priest, that was to him a festive occurrence, and the greatest possible joy; and running to get permission to visit him, he went to his room, and assisted him in boxing up his books, arranging his manuscripts, and packing his clothes, and other articles for the voyage, in his trunks. When the time of taking farewell came, and Abulcher saw the other students weeping and sobbing, because they were about to separate, perhaps forever, from a beloved and amiable fellow-student; he, on the contrary, was replete with joy. He said, "that there was now a new laborer in the vineyard of Christ: one brave warrior more in the ranks of those who were fighting the battles of Israel; and therefore they ought to rejoice, and not to weep, reflecting that, perhaps at the end of his journey, he would find a flock dispersed without a shepherd, which, at the very sight of his face and sound of his voice, would take heart and return immediately to the sheepfold. It was for every one who had any zeal for God the greatest comfort, to hope that the new apostle would enlarge the bounds of the kingdom of God, by converting many infidels, or by bringing back many heretics to the loving bosom of the Holy Church."

But if perchance, any one of his companions was compelled to leave on account of ill health, Abulcher was most afflicted;

and if his heart had not been so full of God, and so entirely conformed to his holy will, he could not have avoided complaining to him affectionately, that when the laborers were so few, and the harvest so vast, he would deprive that poor and abandoned country of all the good that the worthy young man might have accomplished in it. Nevertheless, full of charity as he was, he did not omit to give some holy admonitions and consolations to the invalid, to make him receive with submission this affliction from the paternal hand of God, who directs everything for the best.

In return for his love to his companions, they loved him also with a cordial affection, and they esteemed him highly, knowing that he was a youth entirely given to God, and full of perfection. Merely looking at him incited them to virtue: whence, the author of the memoir says, his companions have declared to me, that merely looking at him, awoke in their hearts a feeling of compunction, and a devout desire to imitate his example. Therefore Abulcher, making use of the authority which his virtue had acquired for him, never let pass an occasion to give them spiritual assistance. He sought especially to moderate those who were of too lively a disposition, and in consequence of this, did not always keep themselves within bounds. If perchance he found any one complaining against the orders of the superiors, he knew how to bring him so dexterously and gently to docility, that subdued by his amiable admonitions, he would return to obedience, and ask pardon for his obstinacy. In literary disputes, where the youthful mind is often so carried away by ardor in maintaining its own opinion, as to offend the opponent by severe words, Abulcher exerted himself to calm the disputants, and by his ascendancy over them, joined to his amiable suavity of manner, he always succeeded in terminating the contention and restoring peace.

These admirable gifts of wisdom, maturity, and observance, induced the superiors to entrust to him a very delicate office, 'for which only the most advanced and exemplary students were selected. Every new comer to the Propaganda, is placed by the Rector in a part of the College separated from that which the other alumni occupy, and there instructed by a companion in the rules and obligations of the College. As long as he remains there, he is called a novice, and his companion holds to him the place of the Master of Novices. Abulcher honored this office greatly, by the exquisite care which he took in the instruction of the youths who were entrusted to him by obedience. He omitted no industry and shunned no fatigue, in planting in their hearts those great virtues which should afterwards bring forth the mature fruits of apostolic perfection; and many of the alumni confessed themselves indebted to Abulcher for that courage and magnanimity of spirit which carried them through the greatest difficulties on their missions.

The memoirs contain a very edifying example of this kind. A youth named John Crispi, a native of the Island of Naxos, in the Archipelago, came from Greece to the Urban College, and on the next day after finishing his retreat, went with the other students to the villa of the College, for recreation. Don Ignazio Oliva was there also, and desiring that Crispi might not diminish on the first day, that fervor which he had acquired by the spiritual exercises of his retreat, he invited him to walk with him alone in a more solitary place. Abulcher having observed this movement, the motive of which he easily divined, followed silently after them, in order to feed his soul on the holy words which fell from the lips of his master. While he was thus taking his delight in hearing him speak of God, Don Ignazio happened to turn his head, and saw him walking noiselessly behind him, step for step, intently listening to his conversation. Knowing very well how much good the holy youth did to the new alumni who were committed to him for instruction in the spiritual life and in observance, he exclaimed: "Oh, here you are, my dear Abulcher, just in the most opportune moment! I give Crispi into your hands, and charge you to instruct him in his duties, and in the holy exercises which are practised in the College." Poor Abulcher blushed deeply in his profound humility, and dropping his eyes in confusion, did not even dare to look up. But as he saw in his confessor Jesus Christ himself, he accepted this commission without answering a word, and devoted himself zealously to the instruction of Crispi.

After Abulcher's death, Crispi, in giving in his testimony to his eminent virtues, narrated minutely what happened that morning at the villa of the College, and I transcribe his own words. "I discovered on that first occasion the abundance of the sanctity which adorned the soul of Bisciarah, in the ready eloquence and sweetness with which he spoke of the things of heaven. He walked with me a long time in the grounds of the villa, explaining to me how sublime and glorious is the vocation of an alumnus of the Propaganda, who is bound by a solemn oath to scatter the shades of error by the light of his teaching. On this account, the ministers of the Gospel are called the lights of the world, which shine for the advantage of poor travellers in the way of salvation. They should be also the loving fathers of their people, leading them on to Christian perfection, not only by their words, but by a becoming exterior, dress, and deportment, and by sanctity of life; otherwise they would render themselves similar to the unhappy men, who, while they preach to others, remain themselves in the number of the reprobate. He finished his discourse, by placing before my eyes the glorious recompense of the true followers and imitators of the apostles, who shine more brightly in the firmament of glory, because they have instructed the people in the truths of the Gospel, and have themselves observed strictly all the precepts of the law." This same alumnus, Crispi, after finishing his studies, was ordained priest, and sent by the Sacred Congregation to the Vicar of the Island of Andros, where with great fervor, zeal, and learning, he guided and instructed his people in the faith, and in good morals.

Abulcher did not limit his charity to the novices alone; but in the pure simplicity of his innocent heart excited all to the love of God. Whence it happened that his companions, from whatever motive they might converse with him, never left him without some good admonitions. He was accustomed at the time of recreation, after exchanging a few words with his companions, to withdraw quietly from their circle, and to walk up and down the corridor as if lost in thought. At the end of it there was a wooden crucifix fixed to the wall, and Abulcher, fixing his eyes on it, was soon, unawares, absorbed in reflecting on the bitter sufferings endured by Jesus for ungrateful men. And in this contemplation, his soul was moved to such deep grief, that his heart palpitated violently in his breast, and unable to control the impetuosity of his emotions, he broke out against his will into groans and abrupt exclamations, which excited his companions to compunction and admiration; although no one ever presumed to disturb him, or call him back to the recreation. Xavier Roll, however, who, as I have said before, loved and esteemed him extremely, observing that this continual meditation was consuming more and more the feeble remnants of his strength, followed him one day as he withdrew from the others, and went towards the crucifix, and drawing him aside, he said to him: "Why will you destroy yourself by such constant application? Why are you always solitary and thoughtful? Come with us, and relax your wearied spirit with some cheerful conversation. Your health is suffering greatly, and if you do not relent somewhat from this rigor, I assure you that you cannot support it much longer." Then Abulcher, with his usual smile on his lips, invited him to walk with him; and with the greatest modesty replied to him: "Oh, *mio caro* Roll, if you knew the sweetness of conversing with God! No; it is not true that the mind is fatigued by it; but so abundant, and so delicious is the sweetness by which it is inundated, that if it suffers it is from inability to support such great joy. Prove yourself, by experiment, if I speak the truth; give yourself to prayer; and taste for yourself how sweet the Lord is. In the beginning, our poor and miserable nature, which is ever inclined towards the earth, endures fatigue it is true, in sustaining herself for a while among celestial things; but by degrees, with the assistance of God, she becomes lighter, and having at length conquered her repugnance to contemplation, she can no longer relish any other food, or take delight in any other occupation."

These memorable words were related by Roll himself after Abulcher's death, to the individual who drew up the relation of his virtues. Thus he went on, and without any thought of playing the preceptor over his companions, by discreetly seizing on every opportunity which came in his way, he produced the happiest results among them. And so abundant and lasting were the fruits of his exhortations and good examples, that, as I find it recorded in the MSS., it seemed to many that God, who in the admirable secrets of his providence had decreed the untimely death of Abulcher, desired to give him the opportunity of gaining in this way greater merits for heaven. God did not will that he should be an apostle in Egypt, where he might have labored so powerfully; but in place of this, he destined him, and filled him with the divine fire of grace, to promote among his companions in a thousand ways, the emulation of the most difficult and sublime virtues. And so completely did he fulfil this intention, that we find it written in the memoir: "We have evident proofs that the virtuous examples which Bisciarah gave to his brethren, and the heroic sentiments which he constantly inculcated on them, did not remain fruitless; for in the letters of the superiors of the missions, we find that his fellow students, now scattered over many portions of the globe, and occupied in the sacred ministry, fulfil perfectly by an exemplary conduct, and a fervent zeal, the duties of their institute, keeping before their eyes, as we may believe, the image and the words of their beloved companion Bisciarah."

CHAPTER VII.

ABULCHER'S EXTRAORDINARY PIETY, AND PERFECT LOVE OF GOD.

IN conclusion, we will add a few words concerning the piety of Abulcher, which the excellent and learned author of his memoir characterizes as "rare and wonderful." In another place, he says that it was constant under every kind of proof. Speaking to the alumni, he writes: "Your blessed brother was endowed by God with the wonderful gifts of an eminent sanctity." Again:— "Every one of you has given a brilliant testimonial of the wonderful sanctity of this student." He does not hesitate to give him frequently the title of "Saint," particularly when, speaking of the witnesses whose testimony was taken, he says: "During many years you were the companions and the admirers of this saintly youth." These things, coming from such an eminently wise and discreet man as Father Ildefonso da San Carlo, ought to have great weight.

In order to treat this subject in an orderly manner, I will speak separately of his devotion to the Virgin Mary, to the Passion of Christ, and to the Blessed Sacrament; and then I will describe the way by which he arrived at that most perfect union with God which is an anticipation of Paradise, and resembles in part the celestial life of those who have already attained eternal beatitude.

We have already described the tender devotion of Abulcher to the Blessed Virgin Mary in his childhood, the fervor and confidence with which he recommended himself to her on his voyage to Rome, and the signal graces which this benignant and clement Queen bestowed on him in return for his filial love and homage. At Rome, in conversation with his companions, he never ceased to speak of Mary. And as his spirit was entirely absorbed in God, and in the love of solitude, his companions, when they were afraid he would leave their company, introduced in an agreeable manner, some topic of conversation relating to the Blessed Virgin. The countenance of Abulcher would kindle immediately, and he would commence to speak of her so fluently and so eloquently, that he could never finish. He adorned her with the most splendid titles, but he made use of none more readily or more frequently than that of Mother. This name, when it issued from his mouth, seemed so affectionate, so joyful, and so brilliant, and he pronounced it in such an ardent manner, with his face all radiant, and his attitude like that of a person in an ecstacy, that he communicated to the others the same ardent love for Mary, and the desire to consecrate themselves unreservedly and irrevocably to her.

If the missions were touched upon, he ascribed all the good which the evangelical laborers accomplished to the protection of the Most Holy Virgin. He often related the miracles wrought by her, which are recorded by ancient and modern writers. He used to say, that to place a mission under the patronage of Mary, and to see it prosper, were one and the same thing. The most contumacious and obstinate minds, the hardest and most savage hearts yield, are softened, are broken, and become mild and tractable. Wolves changed into lambs, lions into playful dogs, hawks made as timid and gentle as doves, such are the wonderful metamorphoses wrought by the sweet enchantment of a glance, a word, an invitation from this celestial empress of hearts; for no one has such a ferocious temper that he can resist the amiable influence of Mary.

Among the titles by which he honored her in a particular manner, he had selected above all others that of Mother of Sorrows; and this for several reasons. The first was, that he was incessantly occupied in meditating on the Passion of Christ, with which the Sorrows of Mary are intimately connected; and by turning his thoughts from one to the other he was more powerfully moved to compassion and grief. He believed also that the love of Mary suffering was most agreeable to her, on account of the natural desire of every one who is in pain, to receive the sympathy of their friends. He saw her alone, at the foot of the cross, desolate, and oppressed with grief, and pitying such great anguish, he desired to keep her company in her solitude, hoping to give her some little relief by this. Finally, to invoke her assistance at that moment when Jesus, taken down from the cross, is resting on her bosom, and she has her eyes fixed on her Son, dead for the love of us, is the sweet means to obtain from her every grace, especially that of never offending God. In a little book in which he wrote down the illuminations he received in meditation, and his good resolutions, it was found written: "I promise to recite every day, with my arms extended in the form of a cross, in honor of the Sorrowful Mary, *Sancta Mater istud agas, Crucifixi fige plagas, Cordi meo valide;* that she may keep me from all occasions of sin, and obtain for me the grace to live always with greater foresight." He often invoked her holy name, which drives away devils, and consoles the afflicted; which is the star that guides us into port, the honey that sweetens every bitter draught, and our only hope in life and death. He had written in his little book: "I place my purity as a sacred trust in the hands of Mary, and promise to recite every day the five psalms in honor of her most holy name, that she may assist me, and deliver me from the snares and assaults of the devil, and preserve me during the whole course of my life faithful and dear to my God."

From various traits of the life of Abulcher, we can see with what deep emotion he meditated on the Passion of Our Lord Jesus Christ. He could not look at the crucifix without his countenance becoming inflamed, and without beginning to sigh and weep through an excess of grief, sometimes even in presence of his companions. The very name of Jesus Crucified would make his heart palpitate: the sight of the wound of his side rapt him away from himself. If the excellent priests of the College wished to kindle in their hearts the love of Jesus

Christ, they had only to visit Abulcher, and bring him to speak of the sufferings of the Saviour. He poured forth such a flood of eloquence, and spoke with such warmth and power of expression, as to draw tears from his hearers, and touched their hearts powerfully, by the deep piety which breathed in his words, and was expressed in his countenance. Frequently the priests did not have to go in search of him, for being extremely desirous to enter continually more deeply into the mysteries of the Passion, he came to them himself, and requested them to explain these to him in all their aspects.

The Passion of Christ spurred him on to labor, to humble himself, to suffer, to overcome himself, and to renounce all attachment to creatures. His continual meditation on the bitter pains of Jesus, say the MSS., not only extinguished in him all desire and curiosity after earthly pleasures, but also inflamed him with a most ardent longing to tread the same path which he saw stretching before him, covered with thorns, and bathed in the blood of his Redeemer. And since he who loves is timid, Abulcher, from the fear of offending God, ran to hide himself in the wounds of his Jesus, certain that the enemy could not touch him in that hiding place. He had written in his little book of resolutions: "I promise to recite every day five Paters Aves and Glorias, in honor of the five wounds of Jesus my Saviour, in order that he may liberate me from every sin, and may command my guardian angel to assist me in all my actions, that I may not use his benefits to offend him, and may always remember that God is present with me in every time and place, observing my actions."

Keeping always before his eyes Jesus scourged, insulted, lacerated, pierced by the thorns, oppressed by the cross, and cruelly nailed to it, he wept over the sins of men, and overflowing with zeal and compassion, animated himself to labor for the conversion of infidels. His desires in this respect were boundless, and embraced the whole world. Egypt was for him only the field where he was destined to labor, and which he loved on that account in preference to the other missions; but in his prayers he demanded the conversion of all heretics, Mohammedans and heathen, even the most savage and unknown nations. Sometimes he complained gently to God that he permitted the saving rivulets of the Blood of Christ to be wasted, and did not irrigate with them those infidel countries, which remain always desolate and unfruitful, and bring forth only thorns and thistles. He could not pacify himself when he thought how the love of Jesus Christ is repaid by such hideous and monstrous acts of ingratitude, especially on the part of sinful Christians.

One day, as the students were enjoying a holiday in a vineyard belonging to the College, on the banks of the Tiber, after dinner was over they were all out in the open air, some playing, some chatting together in groups, and others amusing themselves by walking up and down under the trees. The Swede Roll happened to stroll under an elm tree which overshadowed the bank of the river, and being a light and alert youth, he climbed up the tree, and concealed himself in the thick umbrage, to enjoy the fresh air, and the delightful prospect towards the water. Just as he had seated himself on a large branch, he saw our good Abulcher approaching, with his eyes sometimes turned towards heaven, and sometimes on the surrounding landscape, and finally stopping by the river-side immersed in his thoughts.

Not wishing to be discovered, Roll remained perfectly still, and very soon Abulcher came directly to the foot of the elm tree, and knelt down. He believed himself entirely alone, and therefore raising his eyes to heaven, he gave full vent to the current of his emotions. "Is it possible," he exclaimed, "O Lord God, that men have hearts hard enough to offend you? You are so good, so merciful, so beautiful, and so worthy of love, and yet your beauty and goodness are not sufficient to make you loved! Ah! the meanest creatures have such powerful attractions that they rob you of the hearts of men, and you endure this! To inflame their love, you have descended from the splendor of heaven, and condescended to dwell among them; and men—the cruel wretches—men have rewarded such an excess of love and courtesy, by dragging you to the death of the cross. O God! O my God, pardon such an excess of blindness, and convert all the sinners of the world." As he uttered these words, he fell into a paroxysm of grief, and began to weep and sigh so bitterly, that Roll, out of pity for him, and wishing to liberate himself from his awkward position in the tree, called out to him. The sound of his voice frightened Abulcher extremely; and confused at being overheard in his devotions, he escaped in the greatest haste to another and more lonely place, that he might pour out his heart before Jesus Christ without reserve, and pray to him for the conversion of sinners.

The Prefect Gravio testifies, that having often to pass through the corridor late at night, to visit the sick, or for other duties, he heard the severe blows of the discipline with which Abulcher was flagellating himself, and heard him break out into exclamations and devout affections towards Jesus Crucified, whose image he wore always on his breast, that he might have continually before his eyes, as well as in his heart, the dolorous passion of the Saviour.

In the pains of his sickness he thought of the cross; and when the severest spasms of the disurie, or the paroxysms of coughing, which finally brought him to his grave, tormented him, he fixed his eyes on the crucifix; and the sight of it was such a salutary medicine, that the lamentations died on his lips; his brow, contracted by pain, became serene; his soul was inundated by a sweet peace; and instead of complaints, he uttered the most affectionate words of thanksgiving to his Jesus, who deigned to grant him the grace to share in the sufferings of his cross. And when he saw others suffering, he had no more potent balsam for soothing their pains, than to exhort them to think on Jesus agonizing for love of us.

The idea of that love of Jesus Christ

which induced him, besides suffering so much for us, to give us his entire self in the Divine Sacrament, inflamed the heart of Abulcher with an ardent devotion towards the most Blessed Eucharist. Scarcely had he tasted of it in his first communion at Sethfeh, when its superabundant delights extinguished in him the relish for all except celestial pleasures. The sweetness and fragrance which the immaculate flesh of the Lamb of God diffused in his breast were so powerful, that his frail nature was not able to support them, and he often fainted away after communion. But while his body fell thus into a sweet deliquium, his soul received a new accession of vital force; for the one who loves derives strength from those loving languors, which invigorate the spirit in the same proportion that they enfeeble the body. He could never approach to receive Jesus Christ without bursting into tears. His face glowed, his heart beat violently, and he sighed deeply; and then in an instant the calm of a most profound peace hushed this agitation, his eyes were fixed on heaven with the air of one beatified, and his soul fled away into ecstatic communion with God.

The memoirs speak very often of the change of his countenance, and that appearance of brightness which imparted to him such an attractive expression of joyousness, that the mere sight of him was sufficient to calm every interior disturbance of mind. While he was still a boy in his own country, his intimate converse with God had filled his heart with such contentment that his eyes sparkled, and a modest joyousness was depicted on his countenance, which excited devotion in all those who beheld him. We read of him also, that there ever appeared in him a certain transport of love towards the Blessed Sacrament, which he could not approach without shedding tears, and a sensible heightening of color in his cheeks. So, also, the Prefect Gravio attests, that "Abulcher received from his hands the Divine Redeemer with such devout emotion, that it shone in his eyes and in his countenance, which was entirely inflamed at that moment with a more vivid color than ordinary." .

So ardent was his desire to receive Jesus Christ, that on the days of communion, although he was often ill and suffering, and the cold was extreme, he would always rise from his bed, and go to the chapel with the other students. To see him so pale, weak, and emaciated, and scarcely able to keep himself erect while he walked the few steps from his bench to the altar, was an occasion of great admiration and edification to the others. And when it happened that the physician had ordered him to take some medicine very early, not being able to contain his desire to receive communion, he would beg Don Giovanni Gravio, for the love of Jesus Christ, to say Mass in the chapel before the others were up, and give him communion. And the good Don Giovanni could not have the heart to deny him this request, and witness afterwards his great disappointment.

From this, it is easy to imagine with what careful preparation he approached to receive the Body of the Lord. He prepared himself with profound recollection, commencing with a strict examination of conscience, and an humble confession with many tears. Afterwards, in order to aid himself to awaken the most ardent desires in his soul, he read a little book, in which, say the MSS., he had collected, and transcribed himself, all the most tender and affectionate sentiments which he found in the works of that great master of the spiritual life, Father Louis of

Granada, his favorite author; and he had given it the title of "Meditations to Awaken Fear and Love Before Communion." He also made frequent visits to Jesus in the Blessed Sacrament, and entreated him to purify his heart with the fire of his love, to melt and consume it, and transform it into himself, that he might say with truth: *Vivo autem, jam non ego, vivit vero in me Christus.*

In truth, Abulcher had increased so much by means of the Holy Communion, in the possession of God, that it might justly be said of him, that he lived only from God. God gave him the spirit and the strength to love him more and more, and the more he loved him, the more he prayed for his love with a holy insatiability. He saw him in everything, and loved everything in him, and without him no pleasure had any relish for him, but, on the contrary, was insipid and bitter. While he was still a little boy,

God had given him such a clear knowledge of himself, that the bare thought of God rapt him out of himself into ineffable ecstacies of mind. His ecstacies in the little chapel of Sethfeh, his nightly contemplations on the terrace, and his profound recollection when travelling on foot, on the back of a camel, or in a boat on the Nile, which I have already related, testify to this fact. These wonderful effects were produced in his simple and untaught soul, by the grace of the Holy Ghost, his only master; who trained his pure young spirit to these lofty flights, as the eagle teaches her young eaglets to soar aloft.

During his College life, he increased so much in the divine love, that he no longer seemed to belong to the earth. An eye-witness says, " that the strict union which bound this innocent soul to God, appeared from the circumstance that he was never separated from him or distracted, at any time or in any place." The same person continues: "Let it be considered also, with what fidelity and exactness he corresponded always to the sweet movements of grace and to the divine inspirations, since he had not in the brief course of his life any greater anxiety than to preserve and increase his interior and familiar communication with God by means of prayer. Night and day, God was the only subject of his thoughts, and even in the time of recreation, as we have already seen, he was abstracted and lost in God. As we read in the memoir; " his conversation was entirely in heaven." And Don Ignazio Madaber, a Coptic priest, who became his spiritual director after his removal from the Propaganda to the Convent of Santo Stefano de' Mori, testifies that whenever the conversation turned on worldly topics, he withdrew, " in order not to diminish the flame of that divine fire which burned in his bosom, and not to interrupt the sweet converse which he held continually with heaven."

The desire of embracing every opportunity to converse with God, in order that he might advance every day in the most strict and intimate union of love with him, arrived at such a pitch, that it overcame his extreme repugnance to ask for dispensation from the community exercises. Whence, in the last year of his stay at the College, he often begged permission from the superior to stay away from the recreation and remain alone in his room, that he might enjoy the contemplation of the divine perfections. And his kind superior granted him willingly this permission, knowing well the great advantage which the whole College received from the prayers of Abulcher. The day did not satisfy him, but passed over his head with the greatest rapidity, and was too short to satisfy his thirst for communing with God; and therefore, he employed the long hours of the night in prayer. During these still hours when all was so silent around him, he enjoyed the happiness of Paradise; and such was the plenitude of that torrent of lights and consolations with which the Holy Ghost inundated his heart, that being ill able to contain them, he was forced to break out into sobs, sighs, and colloquies; as we learn from the Prefect Gravio, who used to listen at his door, and from those of his companions whose rooms were adjoining his.

. But I have put my hand to a subject which indeed could furnish ample materials to one who was able to comprehend the mysteries of divine love, and who could delineate and color it with those brilliant hues which the lofty theme demands. Nature, however, cannot reach so far. Therefore in speaking of the love of the saints, we cannot reach further than the bark; for the inner pith of charity is hidden from our eyes, and those who do not love can neither understand nor taste it. The souls who are enamored of God, repose in him and taste of him in solitude and silence, enjoying an ineffable happiness; and the most intense fires are kindled within them, which, unable to find an outlet, are confined and concentrated within themselves. Therefore we will cease to speak of the love of Abulcher to God, and content ourselves with offering up ardent prayers for the grace to emulate him in divine love, and by means of love, to taste of that happiness, of which he said to Xavier Roll, "nothing else which is similar to it can possibly be imagined."

CHAPTER VIII.

OF ABULCHER'S SICKNESS—AND HOW, FOR HIS ALLEVIATION, HE IS SENT TO SANTO STEFANO DE' MORI.

THE relation of the sufferings which this youth endured during his long malady, and of his death in the flower of his years and of his hopes, must excite our pity and compassion. But God, who is admirable in the wisdom of his judgments, wishing to mould with his own hand a soul according to his heart, in order to set him as a model before the young apostles of the Propaganda, conducted Abulcher to perfection by those ways which we have described. And when he saw that he had completed his mission, he called him, as we have reason to hope, to enjoy the fruit of his virtues. Therefore, we may say of him, as of St. Stanislaus Kostka and St. Aloysius Gonzaga: *Consummatus in brevi, explevit tempora multa;* for God computes the years of men, not by the lapse of time, but by the value and worth of their virtue and innocence: *ætas senectutis vita immaculata.* For this reason, the life of the impious, however long it may be and full of magnificent deeds according to the glory of the world, in the eyes of God is destitute of all nobility and merit.

To return to Abulcher. Soon after his arrival in Rome, it was manifest how much his long and tedious voyage, and the bitter cold of the Appenines, had impaired his health. The care of the Rector, F. Sosio, and of the physicians, restored him somewhat, but the winter of Upper Egypt, which is mild, like the soft Italian spring, is very different from a Roman January, especially when the wind from over the mountains, which is very keen and cold, prevails for a long time. Abulcher suffered very much during the first winter, and could never become accustomed to our climate. Besides, he took but little care of himself, his magnanimous heart, and his ardent desire of perfection, always driving him on to the most exact observance of the rules; and if any one out of compassion, admonished him to pay some attention to his health, he answered smiling, that a missionary, being a soldier of Christ, must look for the rigors and hardships of a soldier's life, and that self-indulgence, so far from invigorating the constitution, enervates it the more. This principle was an excellent one, but his strength not corresponding to his good will, he began to suffer greatly from palpitation of the heart and pains in the stomach. As soon as he recovered a little he would return with redoubled eagerness to his studies, and thus he passed the first year of his College life, alternating between illness and convalescence.

After a while commenced the disurie, which increased constantly until it caused him incredible torments. Besides this, he had headaches and sleeplessness, caused by his continual meditations. His exhaustion was so extreme that he could scarcely hold himself upright, and the pain in his breast, and difficulty of breathing, forced him to study in a standing position, which was extremely wearisome. During all his sufferings, he was never heard to utter a complaint, but was so gay and cheerful, that he consoled his companions, who wept and lamented over him. His superiors, who loved him tenderly, were always holding consultations about the means of restoring his health. The MSS. say, that no pains were spared to procure remedies for him, and to preserve a life so precious, and from which such great advantages might be expected for the mission in Egypt. After the first attack of his maladies had subsided, and Abulcher appeared to be revived and re-invigorated, his superiors and companions rejoiced beyond measure, and blessed God for the hope of his recovery. In the spring of 1737, however, Abulcher took a cold, which settled on his lungs, and brought on a violent cough, accompanied by fever, and other new and dangerous symptoms. The physicians exerted all their skill to cure him, but although they succeeded in breaking the first violence of the malady, they could not eradicate it from his system. When the difficulty of breathing caused by the high intermittent fever had subsided, and the other threatening symptoms had partially disappeared, he appeared to be much better. His companions applied communions and public and private prayers for his recovery, begging the Blessed Virgin that she would restore this dear and excellent youth to health, for their consolation and for the benefit of the Egyptian mission. Full of gratitude to his companions for these prayers, he requested them, however, to ask of the Blessed Virgin that he might be purified from every imperfection, and perfectly resigned to the will of God; and that for the rest, they should not trouble themselves about his life or death any more than he did himself.

A few days after he became convalescent, the physicians, after he had entreated them a long time, permitted him to go into the neighboring chapel to hear mass and receive communion. They had not observed, however, that this was no real convalescence but only a mitigated form of the malady, which concealed under a bland appearance the most fatal symptoms. He still retained an obstinate cough, and a quick febrile pulse, from which no medicine could relieve him. Thus he passed the winter, and in the mild weather of spring, the hopes of all revived, only to be entirely overthrown when the hot season arrived, bringing with it to the invalid an extreme languor, a new access of fever, and paroxysms of coughing and hæmorrhage. The Rector Sosio was deeply afflicted and called in other physicians for consultation. It was decided by these, that Abulcher would derive great benefit from a removal to the milder climate of the vicinity of St. Peter's, and he was accordingly removed in the month of September to the Monastery of Santo Stefano de' Mori.

This house stands at the foot of the Vatican Hill, on the Piazza, behind the Basilica of St. Peter, and its windows look directly towards the tribunes of the church. It was formerly given by the Popes to those Ethiopians who resided in Rome as agents for the ecclesiastical affairs of their country, then recently reconciled with the Roman See. The very ancient church of St. Stephen, with its little monastery, has a beautiful garden attached, which stretches towards the Vatican Hill, and extends as far as the turrets of the Leonine Quarter of the city. The Ethiopians remained there, and afterwards the Copts, as long as the missions of Ethiopia and Egypt were flourishing. When, however, Rome was prevented by the bad state of the times from sending more than a few missionaries to Egypt, and the Emperor of Ethiopia commenced a furious persecution against the Catholics of his kingdom, this monastery remained almost uninhabited until this day. The excellent Ethiopian priest, Don Giorgio Galabbada, now lives there alone, as if to watch the sacred spark destined at some future day to break out anew into a splendid flame, and is passing there in solitude and in the peace of the saints the last years of his venerable old age. Born in the kingdom of Tigris, in the errors of the church of Ethiopia, the Holy Ghost infused into his docile mind a light which called him to the faith. He went to Egypt and conversed with the Coptic monks, but found, however, that they also had been seduced from the truth by their own peculiar errors. He resorted next to an Ethiopic bishop, residing in the Thebaïs, and having been instructed by him in the Catholic faith, he made his abjuration in the church of the Latin Missionaries. Shortly after, he went to Asia, and labored for the salvation of souls on Mount Libanus and in Palestine; and after having repeatedly visited Egypt, he was finally called to Rome and employed in the service of the Propaganda, by Cardinal Borgia, who gave him the little monastery of Santo Stefano for a residence.

It was to this house, then inhabited by Coptic monks, that Abulcher was sent by order of his physicians, and was received and taken care of with the greatest affection and kindness by his countrymen. They knew very well what a youth they were receiving as their guest, what edification was to be derived from his every word and action, and of what great virtues they should be the witnesses. And so it was; for Abulcher, as soon as he set foot in this devout monastery, like one who has arrived in a haven of safety, troubled himself no more about the world, but recollecting himself wholly in God, commenced to lead a purely celestial life.

He passed many hours at the window of his cell which looked out upon St. Peter's, and entering the church in spirit, he offered up his heart at the tomb of the Princes of the Apostles. The angels were the sole witnesses of those ardent colloquies, in which he prayed to these glorious saints for the prosperity of the church, for the propagation of the faith in the whole world, for the conversion of sinners, for the necessities of the missions, for strength, light, constancy, and fervor for the missionaries. There, motionless at his beloved window, with his eyes fixed on the church, and rapt out of himself, he drew in those magnanimous sentiments which kindled his bosom and bore his soul aloft toward heaven.

When the monks went to the choir, he went by a little passage near his room to a gallery projecting into the church, to pray with them. This vicinity of the church by means of the little passage gave him the opportunity to go there quietly at all hours, both by day and by night, to adore the Blessed Sacrament and pour out his whole heart before God. When the monks perceived this, and noticed that he was sensibly growing weaker, more through the effect of the love of God, which consumed his soul, than through the progress of his malady, they ordered him to go frequently into the garden, and recreate his spirit with the aspect of the heavens, and the fresh air of the hill. Abulcher, obedient to every sign of his superiors, deprived himself of the delicious retirement of his chamber to walk in the garden. But it was impossible for him to withdraw his mind from God. For the azure of the heavens, the verdure of the earth, the beauty of the flowers, and the song of the birds, were so many friendly voices which spoke to him of God. He often ascended half-way up the hill, and sitting down on a stone, with his eyes fixed on St. Peter's, remained motionless in holy contemplation, while an abundance of the sweetest tears rolled down his cheeks. The monks used to see him from the windows which overlooked the garden, walking up and down under the trees entirely recollected in himself and reciting the chaplet of our Lady. We read in the MSS. that when he went to the garden he had it always in his hand, and recommended himself incessantly to the Blessed Virgin, whom he loved with the tenderness of a child, invoking her assistance at the moment when he should depart out of this life.

A circumstance which occurred on the first day of his arrival at the monastery, shows however, in my opinion, more conclusively than any other proof, the purity of Abulcher's soul, and his solicitude to advance in every kind of perfection. No sooner had he embraced the good monks, and exchanged the first salutations, than he withdrew from them politely, and went to the cell of Don Ignazio Madaber, a religious of great spirituality, fervor, and discernment in the things of God, and throwing himself on his knees at his feet, he humbly prayed him to receive him as a spiritual child, and to guide his soul in the ways of the Lord, saying to him: "Do not refuse, father, to receive under your care a poor little sick lamb, who has cost such fatigue and suffering to the Divine Shepherd, and watch over it with the greatest care, that it may not be lost." And from that day testifies the same Don Ignazio:

"Abulcher came to me every evening with great humility, to manifest the secrets of his heart, all the movements of his soul, and the most indifferent thoughts of the day, in order to have a secure rule in the way of perfection. And he always followed my suggestions with perfect obedience."

In these conferences, the monk Madaber had an ample opportunity to penetrate into the most secret recesses of this angelic soul, and to discover how spotless, and how brilliant with all the ornaments of grace and innocence, it was. He saw, as in the clearest mirror, how pure, simple, and heavenly were his affections; how noble and elevated his thoughts; and how his desires had no other object than God, and God purely for his own sake, the eternal and unchangeable beauty and goodness. He recognized in him the divine conduct of the Holy Ghost, who had taken up his abode in that gentle soul, beautifying it, adorning it, and glorifying it with all the most sublime degrees of virtue, impressing upon it the precious seal of the predestination of the saints, and forming it for the delight of the most august Trinity. In these filial confidences with his master, Abulcher spoke so sublimely of God and of eternal things, that Don Ignazio was overwhelmed with astonishment and admiration. And from his enamored tongue he learned more clearly than ever before, the hidden mysteries of love and of the mutual com-participation of hearts; and the intelligences, the sweetness, the raptures, and the ineffable utterances of the divine harmonies. Whence it happened, that this good monk, both before and after the death of Abulcher, passed such exalted encomiums on his virtue, and wrote of him as a youthful saint, to the faithful in Egypt. He likened him in purity to the most illustrious of the ancient anchorets of the Thebais: he called him an angel on the earth, and he recommended earnestly to his intercession before God, the interests of the Mission of Egypt.

CHAPTER IX.

DEATH OF ABULCHER, AND REMOVAL OF HIS REMAINS FROM SANTO STEFANO DE' MORI TO THE PROPAGANDA—VENERATION IN WHICH HE WAS HELD BY THE ALUMNI.

MEANWHILE, passed away the greater part of the winter of the following year, 1738, and the hectic fever which was wasting the frame of Abulcher could not be subdued by any medical treatment. He became extremely weak, and was often seized by sudden fainting-fits, in which his countenance was shrunken and pallid, large drops of cold sweat bedewed his brow, and he had the appearance of one in his last agony. The monks then ran to him with restoratives, brought him back to his senses, and laid him on his bed. Abulcher had scarcely recovered his scattered senses, when his first aspiration was directed to Mary, whose image was hanging on the wall opposite to his little pallet—then turning with a cheerful countenance towards his comforters, he smiled on them and thanked them for their kindness.

When the Alumni of the Urban College, who came frequently to visit him, were filled with commiseration at his emaciated appearance, he looked on them with a countenance full of gaiety, and said: "Why do you grieve on my account? Suffering is sweet to me, and death most desirable. He who suffers with Jesus, so cruelly tormented for our sins, has reason to render thanks to the good God, who allows him a share in such a great honor, and such great merit." And if any one of his companions strove to entertain him with conversation about the news of the day, he turned the conversation to the things of God, or if he did not succeed in this, instead of being entertained by it, he became sad; and sometimes he said plainly, "My brethren, *the time is short*, and this conversation helps nothing." Therefore, in order to please him, they used to relate to him the most recent intelligence of the Missions, received in letters addressed to the Congregation, or which they themselves had received from their own countries.

Perceiving himself to be growing weaker every day, he redoubled his diligence and fervor, living constantly in prayer to God, and as far as possible, purifying his heart by mortification. Father Madaber, seeing him so reduced, and at the same time so desirous of suffering, made it for him a point of conscience, and told him that in his present state of exhaustion, he ought to relax somewhat from his incessant practices of devotion. But the innocent Abulcher, departing in this thing alone from the counsel of his director, replied to him: "My Father, I have but a short time remaining, in which to live and to merit; leave me then at liberty while the day shines, and until the fatal night arrives in which I can no longer work." And, adds F. Madaber, "he accompanied these words with such an abundance of tears, that he persuaded me to permit him to do as he pleased."

In the beginning of the spring, when the Sirocco and south winds began to blow, which are so strong during the month of March in Rome, Abulcher lost all his remaining strength, and the difficulty of breathing and catarrh became worse. The physicians admonished F. Madaber to watch him carefully, since his lungs were already destroyed, his fever continual, the other symptoms aggravated, and all hope of recovery gone. And although the invalid, ignorant that his disease had arrived at such an extreme, sat up most of the day, as is usually the case with hectic patients, yet, the physician said, things might suddenly take a fatal turn.

The good monk, therefore, concealing the sadness which oppressed his heart, assumed a serene countenance, and began gently to apprize Abulcher of his approaching passage. He began, by saying to him, how beautiful and how noble it is, to commit one's self into the hands of God, and to be ready to give back our life with a joyful mind, to the giver of all good gifts, whenever he demands it. When Abulcher perceived from these words that the hour so desired, and invited by so many sighs, was approaching, his brow lighted up, and not being able to contain the overflowing joy of his heart, he replied to his master in the following words, which he afterwards noted down: "Father, I have always present to my mind the eternal years, and I behold without fear the moment of my release from this earthly prison, trusting in the infinite mercy of my Lord that he will receive me into his loving bosom, to sing his praises with the Blessed in the glorious City of God, through all ages." Having said this he was silent; and going into the presence of the Blessed Sacrament, gave free scope to his exultation, not knowing how to finish blessing and thanking God for this great grace. He chose the Virgin Mary as his mediatrix with her divine Son, and prayed her most fervently to ask from Him pardon in his name, for all his infidelities, to preserve him to the last breath in the love of Him, and of her, His most sweet mother; and that, as the first words which he pronounced as an infant, were Jesus and Mary, so these most sweet names might be the last on his lips in the act of breathing out his soul. He then prayed for the College of the Propaganda, that it might flourish in innocence, in fervor, and in the splendor of all the virtues. He prayed for the missions of the whole world, especially for his beloved Egypt, imploring from God the conversion of the Copts.

Such were the burning affections, with which his soul was more than ever enkindled during these last days of his life; and the Holy Communion which he received very frequently, nourished and fomented them beyond measure. It may be said with truth, that the habit of charity had become so intimately transfused into his soul, that his life was nothing more than a continual ecstacy and rapture in God. Although his malady had reached its final term, Abulcher passed the greater part of the day out of bed, and the pious Solitaries held with him the most delightful conversations on heavenly things. Finally, the evening of the thirtieth of April having come, on which the church celebrates the feast of St. Catherine of Sienna, Abulcher consoled the monks who came to visit him, by speaking for a long time, and with great ardor, of that Seraph of divine love; and when the accustomed hour arrived, they all retired to their cells, leaving him alone with the infirmarian. He also, not anticipating any danger for that night, after he had performed all his accustomed services for Abulcher, and had commended him to God, retired to rest.

Abulcher remained alone; and what he did during that night; what were the effusions of his heart towards God; what sweet tears he shed, and with what loving words he invited the spouse of his soul who was present in his vicinity, to visit him and call him to the kingdom of heaven; these things are known only to God, to the Blessed Virgin, and to the angels who descended to, conduct his blessed soul to their celestial choirs. The next morning, the infirmarian coming at the usual time to bring him his medicine, knocked gently at the door, and receiving no answer, he thought he was still asleep, and went away. After a short time he came again to arrange his room, and opening the window shutters, he perceived him lying on his back on the bed, dressed from head to foot, with his rosary wound around his hands, and clasping the crucifix. His countenance was smiling, his eyes were half open, and fixed on the crucifix with such a loving expression, that he appeared as if absorbed in a sweet contemplation. The infirmarian approached the bed, called him by name, shook him gently to recall him to himself, but finding him cold, perceived that he was dead.

At this sight he shuddered, and ran in breathless haste to call the monks, who came all to the chamber of Abulcher immediately, and could never satisfy themselves with looking at him, such was the brightness and serenity of his angelic countenance. They all wept, but more from a sentiment of tender devotion than from grief. Don Ignazio Madaber was more deeply affected than all the rest, for he knew well what great virtues resided in that immaculate soul. And it was his opinion, that Abulcher, when he felt the first sensations of an extreme faintness which announced his approaching passage, that he might not lose an instant of his precious time, had placed himself dressed in that way on his bed, and recommending his soul to God, had breathed out his spirit, with the names of Jesus and Mary on his lips.

When the blessed death of Abulcher was known in the Propaganda, the lamentation was great, and the benedictions of his name were endless. Every one recalled some beautiful saying or action of him: his piety, devotion, and charity were exalted with the highest praises; and all voices accorded in calling him "an angel of God, a youth of spotless purity, a rare example of modesty and every Christian virtue." They awaited the transportation of his remains to the College with the same impatience with which one awaits the arrival of a most beloved friend after a long and perilous voyage, in order to receive him with the greatest marks of affection and honor. On the evening of the first of May, the Rector of St. Peter's with a number of his priests and the confraternity of Santa Maria in Via, took the corpse from Santo Stefano de' Mori, and brought it to the College of the Propaganda, where the Rector, with the priests of the house, and the students drawn up in ranks within the hall, were waiting to receive it. After the body had been taken into the church, and during the celebration of the exequies, the youths of the College surrounded the catafalque and could never cease feeding their eyes on that beloved countenance on which there still rested a smile which seemed to express his joy at being once more among them. He had nothing of the appearance of death except the pallor; in every other respect he was like one sleeping a most placid sleep, and his countenance expressed a peace, a serenity, and a joy so pure, that the Alumni felt their souls pervaded by a wonderful consolation in looking at him.

Don Ignazio Oliva, the spiritual director, seeing this, and knowing how powerful the example of the good is to awaken a zeal for virtue in the bosoms of all, addressed a short and effective exhortation to the students.—"You see here," he said, "that Abulcher, whom you have loved and admired during life, and who, although now dead, excites more devotion than grief in your bosoms. But to prize virtue without imitating it, is a greater error than not to appreciate it at all. He arrived at such a height of perfection, not with his folded hands, but by valor and constancy. Now he has received a crown from the most just God; but there is no crown without a conquest, and no conquest without a battle; Abulcher fought and conquered, and he has obtained glory, not as a mere gift, but as the reward of merit.

"He preserved his innocence till his last breath; a precious gem which cannot be purchased except at the costly price of abnegation, mortification, and constant prayer. He panted eagerly for the missions; but he understood perfectly the dignity of the apostolic life, and implored of God to grant him the eminent virtues and the sanctity which it requires. To aspire to the missions, and to be at the same time tepid, languid, enervated in the practice of piety, intent on the commodities of life, dissipated in spirit, regardless of obedience and observance, is the same thing as to lie in the face of God, and to betray the most sublime ministry of the apostolate. He who wishes to become an apostle, must hold the wisdom of the world for foolishness, and make himself a fool for Jesus Christ; he must keep himself crucified to the world and the world crucified to him; rejoice in suffering, and endure with invincible courage hunger, thirst, persecutions, insults, calumnies, imprisonment, and death. He who does not find in himself these courageous sentiments, knows nothing, as yet, of the sublime destiny to which he is called. He should excite himself to fervor, and pray to God earnestly, first, that he might know what the apostolic life is; and then, how he should prepare himself worthily for it. Thus acted Abulcher, and now he enjoys with God the fruits of his generous exertions. His former companions ought to recommend themselves to him who was so innocent and so dear to the Blessed Virgin Mary, and beg of him to intercede for them, that they might obtain these great gifts."

These words of Oliva pierced the hearts of the Alumni like burning arrows; and there was not one who did not shed tears and promise to God to imitate the virtues of Abulcher. On the following day, the Office and Mass for the Dead were sung, and after the funeral rites were completed, Abulcher was buried in the church, in the vault of the Alumni. But his memory was not buried with him in the tomb, it lived as a perpetual and delightful reminiscence in the minds of his companions. Their love was not satisfied with his mere remembrance, but every one strove to obtain something which had belonged to him, that he might preserve it as a sacred memorial. They seized, therefore, with avidity on all his manuscripts, pictures, tablets, and every thing else on which they could lay their hands, and happy was he who could carry off something. Those two precious little books in which he had written down with his own hand the graces which he received from God and from the Queen of angels; the illuminations which he received from the Holy Ghost in his meditations; and the resolutions and fruits which he derived from them, were carefully preserved, and finally came into the hands of Father Ildefonso di San Carlo, who made great use of them in drawing up the Memoir of his life.

For the greater edification of all, his portrait was also taken, and the innocent expression, the composed and modest countenance, and the eyes full of piety and fixed on the crucifix, still excite sentiments of the most tender devotion in all who look on it. His picture hangs beside that of Giusto Risgalla Caho, (an Egyptian, and a youth of most pure life,) in this holy retreat, as an example and stimulus for others. The following inscription was placed beneath the portrait of Abulcher, as a perpetual memorial of his illustrious virtues, and his virginal purity:

> **Bisciarah Abulcher Egyptius,**
> MIRA VITÆ INNOCENTIA,
> ET MORUM CANDORE PRÆDITUS, SUI DESI-
> DERIUM ET EXEMPLUM RELIQUIT.
> OBIIT ROMÆ, DIE XXX APRILIS, ANNO DOMINI,
> M.D.CC.XXX.VIII., ÆTATIS SUÆ, XXIV.

Although more than a century has passed since this admirable youth, as we hope, went to enjoy the face of God, I do not know that any one has before undertaken to write and publish his life. But Divine Providence, which disposes all things for its own high ends, would not permit that the MSS. in which were contained the memoirs of the life of Abulcher, should be lost in the various transmutations of the archives of the Propaganda, especially during the invasions of the beginning of the present century, which brought so much distress upon Rome, and threw every thing, sacred and profane, into confusion. These MSS., though somewhat imperfect and injured by the wet, fell ultimately into the hands of Monsignor the Count de Reisach, late Rector of the Urban College, and now Archbishop of Munich; who, during more than six years, labored with great zeal and signal success to promote solid piety among the Alumni; and whose tender love for his pupils, amiable manners, exquisite prudence, and vast learning, have left in the hearts of all a profound sentiment of gratitude and reverence. The company of Jesus having succeeded this distinguished prelate in the government of these virtuous and beloved youth from all the nations of the universe, Monsignor de Reisach, before his departure for Bavaria, gave the said Memoirs to the present Rector, recommending and praising them very highly, as being full of useful instructions for the Alumni of the Propaganda. The Rector finding them full of value and interest, and sufficiently ample to afford materials for a biography, laid the task of writing it during leisure hours upon me. This task, assigned to me by obedience, I undertook readily, animated by the encouragement of Monsignor de Reisach, and also of the illustrious and learned Monsignor Mai, Secretary of the Sacred Congregation (afterwards Cardinal Mai), who has always had deeply at heart, the spiritual profit of the Alumni of the Propaganda, and who was very desirous that I should write the life of this youth, as one of the choicest fruits of the Urban College, and a most noble example of piety and innocence, well calculated to excite the virtuous and well-disposed young men of the College to a generous emulation.

Thus it pleased God, after the lapse of a century, to make manifest for his own greater glory, the eminent virtues of his servant. The humility of his servants causes them to be intent only on concealing themselves from the eyes of the world in solitude, regarding themselves as vile, and careless of human praise. But on the other hand God, who has said that *he who humbleth himself shall be exalted*, competes with them in liberality and munificence. While they, in order to please him, conceal the most splendid virtues with the greatest care, and aspire only after contempt, insults, and every kind of opprobrium; God on the contrary, changes all the contumely which comes upon them into honor and glory. And always solicitous for their honor, he often awakes even their cold ashes from the silence of their sepulchres, revives the memory of their virtues among men, and inspires them to offer them solemn veneration, to practice devotions in their honor, and to resort with confidence to their patronage.

I, for my part, profess myself to be a venerator and a great admirer of this angelic youth; and the more this work has grown under my hands, and I have learned more and more of his purity, innocence, and charity, the more I have felt myself excited to compunction, love and reverence. I have often recommended myself to his intercession with Mary, and always to my singular consolation. I believe that I have also obtained through him a most signal grace, which I had long prayed for with many tears. May he condescend to accept in heaven the homage of my grateful mind, and enkindle in my bosom that ardent love for God which ever burned in his own heart, that I may inflame also the hearts of these young apostles, from whose zeal, fervor, and sanctity so many unhappy nations are awaiting their salvation!

Obtain for me also, O blessed Abulcher! the translator of this book, and for all who shall read it, the same grace; that the love of Jesus and Mary may burn in our hearts while we live, and the sweet names of Jesus and Mary be the last sound that trembles on our expiring lips!

FINIS.

Printed by BILLIN & BROTHER, 20 North William St., New York.

Quæ narrantur in hoc libello Vitæ Abulcheri Bisciarah, et miracula, prophetias, revelationes, aliaque hujusmodi, sapiunt, humana dumtaxat auctoritate, non autem. Divina nituntur; atque ita fideas sit penes auctorem, juxta Decretum SS. Urbani VIII., datum die V. Junii, M.DC.XXXI.

www.ingramcontent.com/pod-product-compliance
Lightning Source LLC
Chambersburg PA
CBHW022127160426
43197CB00009B/1184